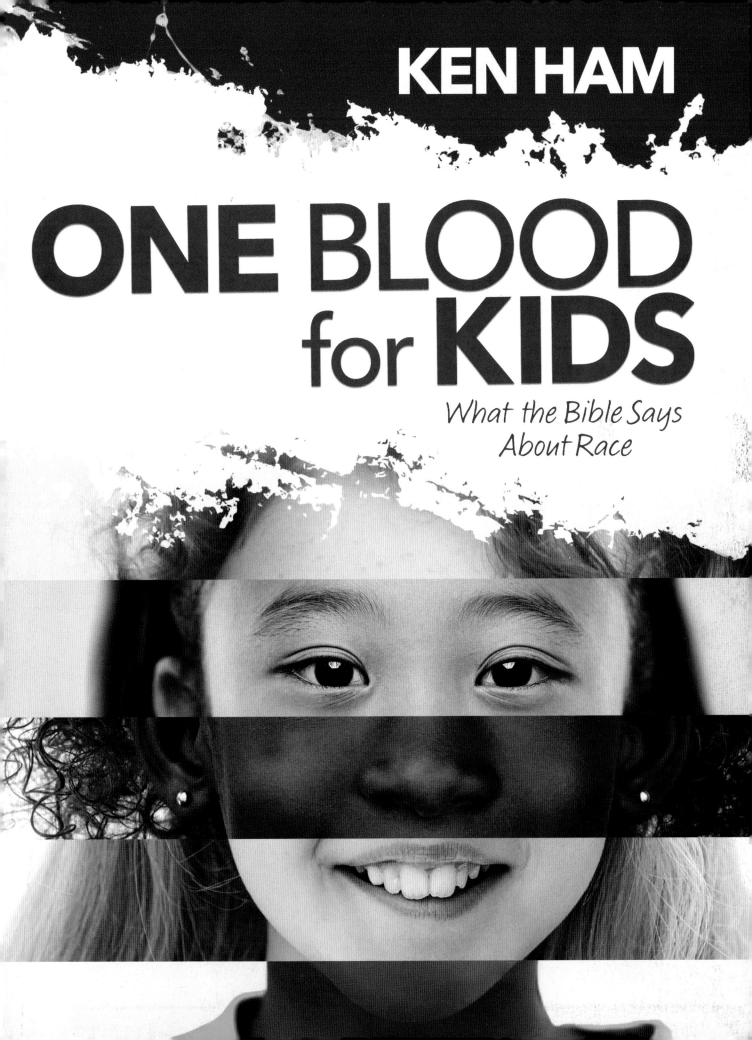

KEN HAM

ONE BLOOD
for KIDS

*What the Bible Says
About Race*

First printing: August 2018
Second printing: February 2019

Master Books®, P.O. Box 726, Green Forest, AR 72638

Master Books® is a division of the New Leaf Publishing Group, Inc.

ISBN: 978-1-68344-120-5
ISBN: 978-1-61458-676-0 (digital)
Library of Congress Number: 2018952292

Cover by Diana Bogardus

Please consider requesting that a copy of this volume be purchased by your local library system.

Printed in China

Please visit our website for other great titles:
www.masterbooks.com

For information regarding author interviews, please contact the publicity department at (870) 438-5288.

Note to Parents—Why It Matters

Today's world is focused on race and the divisions that so-called science, culture, or hate create. It is important for children to understand that God's Word gives us the true history of life, so we can build a truly Christian worldview and address this issue correctly. Races (as used in today's world) and racism are man-made concepts that were never based on the biblical foundation God set forth in Genesis. The most important takeaways from this book are:

→ We are all uniquely and specially created by God.

→ We are all part of one race, the human race, and racism is a sin.

→ Jesus died on the Cross as our Savior to offer His free gift of salvation for those of any tribe and nation.

The biblically based worldview of mankind is simple—Adam and Eve, the very first human beings, were created by God, and every person who has ever lived or will live are descendants of this couple. While we may look a little different on the outside, speak differently, or have different cultural backgrounds, we are all still children of the first man and first woman. Any of these minor differences we see are superficial—and any negative or racist thoughts falsely based on these differences are sinful.

In this book, the reader will take a spiritual journey to discover the real history of man, the connections between us, and how the variations of our skin tones and so on reflect the creativity of our Creator, who lovingly fashioned us in His image.

God Loves You!

Do you know you are a Special Creation of a Loving God?

You are special.

You are unique.

There is no one in the world just like you.

God knitted you together in your mother's womb (Psalm 139:13).

And He created you for a purpose—something only you can do.

God never makes mistakes.

He knew you can do what He wants you to do.

You may look like your mom or dad, or even some other person in your family, but you are still unique and bear the image of God.

God loves each and every one of us. And while we may all look different, think differently, or live in different cultures, we are all still His special creations.

We are always loved by Him.

But because of sin, we sometimes don't do what God wants us to do or live like He wants us to live. When we disobey God, that is a result of our sin. Even when we sin, God still offers us His grace.

He wants us to love Him and obey and live the way we should according to the Bible.

When we lie, we sin.

When we cheat, we sin.

When we look at people who are different from us and hate them for looking, sounding, or being physically different than we are, this is sin.

When you don't like someone because they are from another culture, or they are deceived into believing a false religion, or they have a different skin tone, that is bigotry and racism. And both of these are a sin.

We are created to be beautiful...and unique.

Remember, God created everyone—to be different in many ways, to be special, but all equal before God as His image bearers.

But sometimes, people forget that. They make terrible and hurtful assumptions about people who are different than they are. If they do this, it is a sin. If you do this, you sin.

We are one race—the human race.

The Bible tells us in beautiful detail how the human race was created, and how sin first entered the perfect Creation. As we learn more about that, we will also learn how science is helping us to know why we look different from one another, what makes us unique, and how the more we know, the more the truthfulness of the Bible is confirmed.

We are one race, one blood.

#set the
TONE

God made
you in His
image—
beautiful and
wonderful.

Our World Today

If I were to ask you which race you belong to, what would your answer be? How many races of people do you think there are?

Some say there are many races. Charles Darwin, the man who popularized the idea that people supposedly evolved from ape-like creatures, also helped to foster terrible ideas of racism. Sadly, his false and destructive ideas, based on his belief in the evolution of man, have caused some people to look down on other people that have different skin tones than their own.

In our modern scientific age, scientists studying human DNA looked at human genes, using people from all around the world, and discovered that there is only one race of humans. Actually, this confirms over and over again what the Bible teaches about the human race—though sadly, many scientists who reject God's Word don't want to say this. All humans belong to the one human race!

The Bible gives us lots of details about the origin of the human race, and events of human history down through time. That's because the Bible is the true history book of the universe. This history has been given to us by God in His Word so that we will understand the truth of how the universe and all life, including humans, came into being.

But I want to take you on a journey—a journey that begins with the first human who ever existed. It's a journey about human beings that, on the basis of the true history of the world as recorded in the Bible, can be divided into seven different biblical/spiritual "races" that are all part of the one human race. Are you wondering what this has to do with the racism we see today?

The Bible has the answer for many of the problems in our world—and by understanding the real history of the human race, you will understand cultures, when science was misused to promote racial inequality/problems and what God expects from us in how we treat each other—no matter how different we may look. It also tells us why God's truth is the only real answer to battling racism because it targets the heart of a person—something laws, education, and social rules cannot do. When you understand what makes us all the same, you will no longer see just the differences!

Which of the seven spiritual "races" are you a member of? Let's find out.

7 Spiritual "Races" in the Bible

CREATED RACE

FALLEN RACE

RESCUED RACE

DIVIDED RACE

SAVED RACE

LOST RACE

LAMB'S RACE

Isaac

Abraham

Shem

Did you know that you are related to the first man and woman God created? The history of every family on earth today, including yours, can be traced back to Adam and Eve.

Ham

Noah

Japheth

Adam

Eve

who?	God (who exists in eternity)
what?	God created everything, including the first people—Adam and Eve.
where?	Today no one knows where Eden was originally because Noah's Flood destroyed the earth, but the Bible gives us a clear description of Eden in Genesis 2:8-14.
when?	Around 6000 years ago, God created time, space, the earth, plants, animals, man—everything that exists. There was nothing before God created it. God exists in eternity and created time for us to live in. Genesis 1 and 2 tell us details of the creation.
why?	God created us for His glory.

God created Adam and Eve just as stated in the Bible; the "monkeys to man" idea is not true. Humans have always been human.

Created RACE

The Bible tells us that the first member of the human race was created on the sixth day of creation about 6,000 years ago. The first human being was a man named Adam. Genesis 2:7–15 tells us that Adam was formed by God from the dust of the ground and that God breathed into his nostrils the breath of life and he became a living, breathing human. These verses also explain that God planted a garden eastward in a region called Eden. In this garden, God made beautiful trees and plants that bore delicious fruit.

After this incredible act of creation, God instructed Adam to name the animals He brought to him. The reason God did this was to show Adam he was alone. In all of the new earth, there was no living thing created in the special way Adam was, being woven together in the image of God. God made it clear to Adam from the beginning that he was different. He even gave him the job of naming the animals to show him that he was actually in charge of them. Adam then set out to accomplish this mission and named the cattle, birds of the air, and every beast of the field. Through this work, God not only introduced Adam to his varied and marvelous creation, but naming the land-dwelling animals God brought to him also allowed Adam to see that he was, in fact, very different from them.

One of the biggest reasons for this difference is because God "created man in His own image; in the image of God He created him" (Genesis 1:27). For example, as humans, we are able to speak, write, appreciate music and art, reason, and know what's right and wrong. While many of us may love our pets and the different animals we see at the zoo or in the wild, it's clear that animals cannot do these things in the way we as humans do.

#set the TONE

People can create art and music. Animals cannot do things the way humans can.

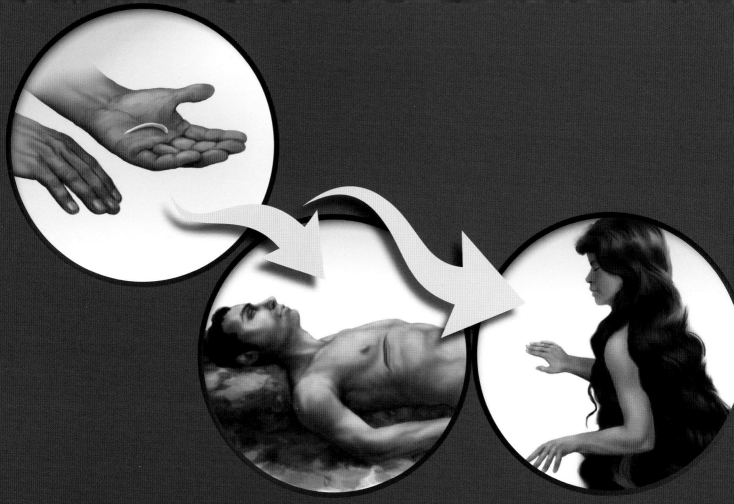

God created mankind specially. Man did not evolve from ape-like creatures as Charles Darwin had said and as students are taught in most schools. Animals were simply not created in God's image.

After Adam recognized he was not just an animal (even though he—like each of us—had a body that was designed similar to mammals), God made the first woman—the second member of the human race. Genesis 2:18–22 tells us that after God created Adam, He said it was not good for man to be alone. So, He caused Adam to fall into a deep, deep sleep (like people do when they have surgery today) and he took one of his ribs from his side, and from that rib he created woman. God is all-powerful so this would have been easy for God to do. After Eve was created, God introduced her to Adam. Adam named her Woman (and eventually in Genesis 3, Eve) because she was to be the mother of all humans to come.

Genesis 2:18–24 also describes the significant moment when God created the very first marriage. When God brought Eve to Adam, He created the first marriage—one man and one woman. Many in today's world try to claim that marriage can be between two men or two women (or any number of men and women). However, the first marriage in Genesis makes it clear that marriage is only between one man and one woman—anything else is against what God's Word teaches.

CULTURE → Marriage: One Man, One Woman

We learn from the Bible that when Adam was first created, he was alone—no other human beings existed. He didn't know he was alone until after he named animals that God brought to him and he saw there were none like him—none made in God's image. But God had a plan for Adam—a plan to create someone for him—and create the first marriage.

When God Made Marriage

While God formed Adam from the dust, Eve had a very different creation. She was formed from a part of Adam himself—his rib. She is the completion of Adam, understanding he was alone and God creating a woman (his wife) for him—a divine plan for companionship—to finish the Creation. God made the first two people male and female.

The Special Creation of Eve

God created everything out of nothing during the Creation Week—including animals and plants, and the high point of creation—Adam and Eve. This is the point where each of our own family histories begin.

Multiply... Why?

From this first couple, many generations of people would be born. Each person would be unique and look slightly different from one another—this includes many variations in skin tones from the original medium brown shade of Adam and Eve. No matter what we look like, we are all made in God's image. Do you realize what that means? You are uniquely made in the image of an all-knowing and loving Creator God. The world, our culture, often wrongly defines us and our value based on what we look like or how much stuff we own. But God created us all equal and offers the free gift of salvation to all people through Jesus' sacrifice for us.

Adam knew God had created his wife from his side. Because God made Eve, Adam no longer had to be alone. Because she was made from him, we know that God intended woman and man to be together. God defines marriage in another important verse in Genesis 2:24 when he describes that when a man and woman get married, they leave their families and start a new family together.

This verse was actually quoted by Jesus Christ; Jesus is God who took on human flesh to become "the God-man." In the New Testament when Jesus was asked about marriage, He answered by quoting from Genesis as He taught that marriage was one man and one woman. Jesus echoes that a man and woman will both leave their families and become one family on their own. He also says, "So they are no longer two but one flesh. What therefore God has joined together, let not man separate" (Matthew 19:6). This verse is important as it shows that marriage is a divine and holy union that God arranges.

Now some Christians have tried to take Darwin's ideas about man evolving from ape-like creatures and say that God made Adam and Eve by using the process of evolution. But people who believe in evolution teach that the woman came from a supposed ape-woman, and the man came from a supposed ape-man. But the Bible states clearly that Adam was made from dust, and the first woman was made from Adam—from his side.

If God made man using evolution, then that would mean the "dust" God made Adam from must really be the supposed ape-man. While this idea is believed by some people, if we follow God's Word this idea just doesn't make sense.

You see, later on in the Bible, we learn that because of Adam's sin, he would die and return to dust. As we all know, when humans die they return to dust—they don't return to some ape-like creature! Scripture tells us this specifically in Genesis 3:19. The Bible states that humans will live, eat, and work until we all return to the ground and dust we were once made from. While this isn't the happiest part of God's Word, there is comfort in knowing that God had a plan from eternity to deal with our sin problem and conquer death, so we can live with God forever in Heaven. From the dust we were created and to the dust we will once again return because of our sin. While death is scary, we also know that because of Jesus we have a sure hope in our life after death (but we'll talk about that more in our next chapter).

As Christians, we must be very careful when we read the Word of God. God tells us clearly in the Bible about the creation of man and woman—the man was created directly from dust, and the woman was made from his side (from Adam's rib). Genesis is written as real history. The Bible means exactly what it says. The Bible does not describe the process of evolution, so we know God didn't use evolution to create the first man and woman. It is important to understand these basic ideas, so we are able to build our firm foundation on real biblical truth. Without a firm foundation, the simple and meaningful truths (like creation) can come under attack, and we can lose our way in the waves of what the world around us wants us to believe.

If Adam and Eve were both middle brown (AaBb, see chart on p. 21), they would have produced children with a wide range of skin tones—which is what we see in our world today. Suddenly, all of us being one race doesn't seem so complicated![1]

Adam, Eve, and their children all had the genetic instructions that allowed the many different skin tones we see today.

SCIENCE → Secrets of Science—The Regenerating Rib!

Eve was created from a rib taken from Adam. This doesn't mean that boys have one less rib than girls. It just means that God knew something about our bodies that science is just starting to understand—that the rib is capable of regenerating, or growing back by itself. A 2014 medical study found that if a rib was removed from a person and the membrane that surrounded the rib (called "perichondrium") was left and surgeons closed it up, the rib bone could regenerate itself within a few months. Science is only showing us what God already knew![2]

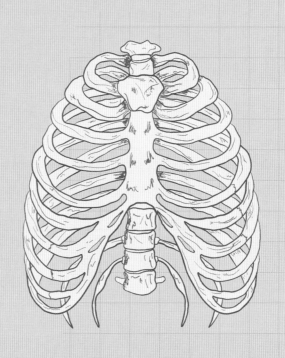

Now after God had finished creating the earth, universe, and life itself (including the first two people), we read in Genesis 1:31 that God looked around and saw everything He had created as "very good."

Looking around at the chaos of today's world, we know that something big has happened to cause the world to change. We see death, disease, terrible events like earthquakes and hurricanes, and evil people acting in horrible ways. So, what happened? How did the created race (the first race) that God saw as "very good" go so bad?

We find out when we understand the second race—the Fallen Race.

Related Scripture List:
Genesis 1:26-27
Genesis 1:31
Genesis 2:7–15
Genesis 2:18-22
Genesis 2:23-24
Genesis 3:19
Matthew 19:4-6

Fallen RACE

Remember when God finished creating the universe and all life? At the end of the six days of creation, He rested and said that all of creation was "very good" (Genesis 1:31). But we know our world is not the perfect one that we read about in the beginning of Genesis. That's because man sinned and fell from God's grace. In this chapter we will explore the fallen race of man and how sin infected God's creation. And how sin has caused a problem with how some people view each other.

Did you know that before the fall of man, Adam and the animals in the Garden of Eden were vegetarians and only ate plants? In Genesis 1:29–30 God explains that He gave them every plant and tree that bears seeds as food for not only man, but also for every bird and beast He created as well. Meat wasn't even given to man as food until after Noah's Flood, which was 1,656 years after sin and death first entered the world.

Before the fall of man, the earth looked a lot different. Life itself changed physically after Adam and Eve sinned. Genesis 3 also tells us that even the animals and the ground were cursed. Verse 18 states that thorns came into existence after sin and the curse.

Now you might be thinking, "What difference could these thorns make?" But even a little detail like when thorns entered the world, as well as the diets of man and animals, gives us important clues about the timeline of sin as well as the age of the human race.

Today, many people believe in an idea that does not make a lot of sense and that is the belief of a very old earth—an earth that has been around for supposedly millions of years. This idea came from the belief that fossil layers were formed very slowly. They also believe that this gradual layering occurred before the existence of man.

#set the
TONE

Sin changed everything on our perfect world.

Sickness and death in the created world were the direct result of the Fall of Man.

So, when Christians wrongly believe in an earth that has been around for millions of years, they are really saying that the fossil layers with all the dead animals in them were laid down before Adam was created.

But a big problem with this idea is that the fossil record contains fossil thorns. Thorns that, according to the belief of evolution, must be hundreds of millions of years old. But how could these thorns be so old if they didn't exist until after Adam sinned, as the Bible teaches?

These fossil layers also contain evidence of animals that ate other animals. These animals had bones in their stomachs, as well as other fossils with teeth marks on bones. This would mean animals were eating each other before they were turned into fossils. But according to the Bible, animals ate only plants originally and didn't eat each other before sin. Because of the timeline God lays out in Genesis, we know these fossils had to be formed after Adam sinned.

These rock layers also have fossil bones showing diseases in them such as brain tumors, cancer, and arthritis. But if these existed before Adam sinned, then it would mean diseases were a part of that original "very good" creation. God would never call diseases of any kind "very good." This means the fossils could not have been formed over millions of years before Adam. They had to be made sometime after Adam sinned.

You may be wondering, "If the earth isn't millions of years old, how exactly did the rock layers with the fossils form?" Because bloodshed, disease, suffering, and thorns came after sin, we can know with full certainty that the fossil layers had to be formed after sin too. But how? What could have created the conditions necessary for these fossils to form after sin? How about a great cataclysmic event? Noah's Flood covered all of creation and would have formed lots of layers of rock with fossils all over the earth. Of course! Noah's Flood formed most of the fossil record.

With our timeline for creation settled, let's zero in on the fallout that occurred after the first sin. The biggest consequence we all know too well is death. Now did you know the Bible calls death an "enemy" (1 Corinthians 15:26)? But when did the first death actually happen? Well, first of all, Adam and Eve were told they would now die because of sin. However, when God clothed Adam and Eve with coats of skins after they sinned, we believe this to be when the first death occurred. Because of sin, the death and bloodshed of an animal was required by God for the forgiveness of sin. But why does God require bloodshed and death? God's Word tells us that without the shedding of blood there is no forgiveness of sins (Hebrews 9:22), and that the life of a creature is in the blood (Leviticus 17:11). Because Adam sinned, a payment for that sin was needed. As we know, the consequence God gave for committing

Wait a minute—didn't people evolve from ape-like creatures?
No—let's look at the DNA evidence:

DNA Don'ts	DNA Do's
Humans evolved from a shared ancestor with the apes.	Humans have genetic differences God created so we won't all look the same—but we are all 100% human!
	Humans and chimps have millions of genetic differences. Chimps are animals. Humans are different than the animals.
Question: Are humans and apes very similar to each other?	Answer: They aren't. The Bible tells us that man was created in God's image, animals were not. God had Adam even name the animals He brought to him to show he was different.

sin is death. Because of the selfish choices Adam and Eve made (and the choices we all make when we sin, because we are descendants of Adam and Eve, we are all the same family—Adam's race), death and bloodshed were needed to pay for that sin. The skin of an animal was given to Adam and Eve as clothes and served as a reminder of the sin they had committed when they disobeyed God. It was also a reminder that God had a solution to our sin problem.

Genesis 3:21 describes the first blood sacrifice of those animals as a consequence for the wrong actions of Adam and Eve. This makes a lot more sense when we apply this to who we know is coming—the Messiah, Jesus Christ, who was the blood sacrifice "once for all" (Hebrews 10:10–14) when He shed His blood on the cross and was raised from the dead.

The Israelites sacrificed animals over and over again, as a picture of what was needed to pay for sin. But Hebrews 10:4 tells us that the blood of animals can't take away sin. We are made in the image of God. Animals were not made in God's image, and humans are not related to animals. That's why we needed a perfect human sacrifice to take away our sin.

It is important to understand that if death and bloodshed existed before sin, then it makes no sense why God said blood had to be shed to pay for sin. If sin hadn't happened yet, there simply would not be any death and bloodshed because these were consequences that happened after the first sin. Also, if there were death, disease, bloodshed, and suffering before sin, then sin itself would be God's fault—not our fault. But all the horrible things in the world are our fault because we are sons and daughters of Adam—we're all members of the created human race. And when Adam sinned, we all became

Related Scripture List:
Genesis 1:29-30
Genesis 1:31
Genesis 3:18
Genesis 3:21
Leviticus 17:11
Romans 5:12
1 Corinthians 15:22
1 Corinthians 15:26
Hebrews 9:22
Hebrews 10:4
Hebrews 10:10-14

sinners together. We are the true cause of death and suffering in the world. It wouldn't make sense for God to say there had to be death as a sacrifice for sin if He allowed disease and death to exist over millions of years before Adam was even created.

Another big question people ask is how Christians can believe in a loving God with so much death, suffering, disease, and "bad" in the world. The correct answer is that because of Adam's sin, our Holy God had to judge sin with death. God is righteous and good. He cannot be in the presence of sin. We alone are to blame for all the bad conditions, events, and circumstances that happen in our "very bad" world. Because God knew Adam would turn away from Him, God made a loving plan to rescue humanity from sin and death and our souls from being separated from Him forever in a place called hell.

Because we are a fallen race, that means that we have fallen away from God. It means that when our bodies die our souls are cut off from God forever. But God wants us to spend eternity with Him. That's why He stepped into history in the person of His Son (as the babe in a manger), to become Jesus Christ the God-man. He became the perfect man by never sinning. Only God could do that! And He did it for us, so He could pay the price for our sin. Romans 5:12 tells us that sin entered the world through one man (Adam) and spread to all men. 1 Corinthians 15:22 explains that in the same way that sin infected all men through the selfish action of one man, it is conquered through the selfless sacrifice of another. Through Jesus' death and resurrection, we are set free!

Because Adam brought sin and death into the world another man would need to pay the price to remove that sin. But it would have to be a perfect man, not a sinner. God's solution was to send His Son. Through Adam's sin came death. Through the death and Resurrection of the Lord Jesus, we can receive the free gift of salvation, so we can live with our loving Creator forever. That's why Jesus is called the "last Adam." Jesus takes the place of the first Adam, so we can have eternal life with God. That's why it is so important we receive this free gift of salvation.

As the fallen race, we have "fallen" away from the "very good" we were created to be. Because of this sin we are separated from God. Understanding this problem also helps us understand why most of Adam's race became so wicked in the time of a man named Noah. And understanding the fallen race also helps us understand (as we will see later on) why certain people treat some humans as if they are of less value than others instead of understanding we are all members of the same human race. We are all equal before God, all sinners, and all in need of salvation. It's so important to understand that the solution to the sin problem (Jesus) is for everyone—for all tribes and nations. So now we come to the next "race"—the "Rescued Race."

#set the
TONE

God has a solution to our sin problem.

SCIENCE→ The Science of Skin Tones

It's all about the melanin!

Have you ever wondered why people have different skin "colors"? It's all about the science of skin tones. There aren't different "colors," only variations of skin tones based on a person's level of melanin (the main pigment) in their skin.

Melanin is a protein that is found in all human skin (except people who do not have melanin, known as albinos) in two forms: eumelanin (brown and black hues) and pheomelanin (red and yellow hues). Melanin is produced by melanocytes, and the amount you can produce is determined by your genetics (from your mom and dad). When you get a suntan, you are starting the production of melanin in response to the sunlight. God created us to produce melanin to protect us from ultraviolet light and produce the Vitamin D we need.[3]

The Layers of Human Skin

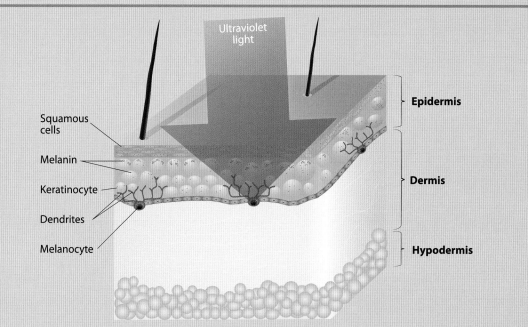

Ultraviolet light

Squamous cells

Melanin

Keratinocyte

Dendrites

Melanocyte

Epidermis

Dermis

Hypodermis

Melanocyte

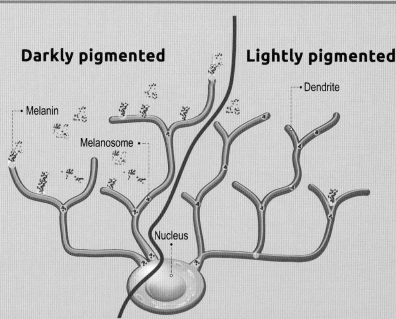

Darkly pigmented

Lightly pigmented

• Dendrite

• Melanin

Melanosome •

Nucleus

SCIENCE → Just One Generation!

What's even more amazing is that it doesn't take a long, long time to see many variations in skin tones—it can happen in just one generation! Such variations are seen within families all the time![4]

Mother

	AB	Ab	aB	ab
AB	AA BB	AA Bb	Aa BB	Aa Bb
Ab	AA Bb	AA bb	Aa Bb	Aa bb
aB	Aa BB	Aa Bb	aa BB	aa Bb
ab	Aa Bb	Aa bB	aa Bb	aa bb

Father (left axis)

AABB Only dark   **aabb** Only light

This truth is even more pronounced when it comes to what are known as "mixed twins"—fraternal twins born into families where the mother and father have different skin tones and different versions of genes called alleles that help determine skin tones. Mixed twins have the genetic potential for high levels of melanin and low levels of melanin. Sometimes one twin will genetically take after one parent while the other twin takes after the other parent. This creates what are sometimes known as "black and white" twins—though this description is not accurate when we know the truth of how genetics and skin tones work. Such twins can also result from couples who could be described as both being middle brown (having a mixture of such alleles as described above). We will learn more about how other factors impact the science of skin tones in upcoming chapters. For example:

"...Now let's see what happens when human beings are separated into isolated groups by barriers such as geography, culture, or language (such as at the Tower of Babel in Gen. 11). If those with very dark skin (AABB) migrate into the same areas and/or marry only those with very dark skin, then they only have capital A and B genes to pass on, and all their children will have very dark skin. Similarly, parents with very light skin (aabb) can have only very light-skinned children, since they have only a and b genes to pass on."[5]

#set the
TONE

Freckles appear when sunlight affects an area of skin resulting in an increased amount of melanin and pigment-producing cells called melanocytes!

There were 1,656 years between the Fall of Man and the birth of Noah's first son before the Flood.[6] We are also told in the Bible that many of these people lived for a very long time, much longer than people do today. We really don't know for sure why they lived such long lives. It may have been due to genetic factors, the environment, or less disease.[7] So how many people were there—and what did they look like?

Even if the population of people were low (it could have been thousands or millions), there would still be a lot of diversity among the descendants of Adam and Eve. Children don't always look exactly like their parents or siblings. Though you may resemble someone else in your family, you are still uniquely you.

If the population were high, possibly from 750 million to 4 billion at the time of the Flood, there would be even more diversity in the pre-Flood population.[8] This didn't end with the Lord's judgment on the earth in the form of the Great Flood. Noah's family of eight people were enough to keep the genetic pool strong enough to produce all the variations we see today. That's why at the Ark Encounter (Arkencounter.com) Christian-themed attraction, Noah and his family are depicted with varying skin tones.

Noah's Ark would not only save the animal kinds, but also the future of mankind as well through the survival of his own family.

Rescued RACE

The Bible tells us that Adam and Eve had many children, including the three specially named in the Bible—Cain, Abel, and Seth. In total, Adam lived to be 930 years old. Can you imagine all the adventures he had in all those years? Jewish tradition suggests that he may have had as many as 33 sons and 23 daughters. While we don't know the exact number of children they had, we do know they had a very large family.

Remember, God only made one man and one woman to be the head of the one human race. Because Adam and Eve made up the only two members of the world's first family, when their children grew up there were no other families for them to marry into. So, when it was time for them to start their own families, they had to marry a relative. Cain, the first son of Adam, most likely married his sister. Now, this may seem really crazy to us today. Keep in mind that way back then (about 6,000 years ago) close family members could marry each other— provided it was one man and one woman. Many years later, God changed this rule and told Moses that people were no longer to marry close family members. We follow this command today because if close family married, with all the mistakes in our DNA that now exist in our bodies because of sin (resulting from the fall of man), there could be disease and defects in the bodies of their children. Now when we marry, we marry someone not so closely related to us.

Adam and Eve's children and their children began to increase in number, and they spread out all over the earth. But remember that these children were descendants of the "fallen race." As time went on, the sin inside them made them more and more wicked. About 1,600 years after Adam and Eve were created the human race as a whole rejected God. Genesis 6:5–8 explains just how evil the hearts of man became. Without God, the human race spiraled into the depths of what we can only imagine must have been a true nightmare. Out of all the people on the earth, there was only one man (with his family) who still followed God. His name was Noah.

#set the TONE

Mankind would reject God except for Noah.

From Noah's three sons and their wives would come many, many more over time, including those living today; even with the destruction from the Flood, there was enough genetic variation in Noah's family for all the skin tones we see today.

Every human being on the earth had given into the wickedness in their own hearts, but Noah and his family, because of his righteousness before God, were spared from God's judgment. God took mercy on Noah's wife, their sons, and their wives. As a result of man's cruelty, malice and all-out evil, God sent the judgment of a Flood that would cover the entire globe and destroy all of mankind.

God also used the Flood to separate those who believed in Him from those who didn't. Hebrews 11:7 tells us that God warned Noah about the Flood many years before the first rains even began to fall. Because of Noah's faith in God, he believed Him and prepared the Ark to save himself, his family, and the animals of God's creation. This is important because it would be easy for us to take for granted the enormous size of the task Noah had to accomplish. This was not a part-time hobby. Building the Ark would most likely take many years and be a full-time job for Noah and his family. It would take incredible daily faith to believe in the coming Flood and give the time and energy to build the Ark.

Noah had faith, and God gave him instructions about the size of the Ark, as well as the type of wood he would use to build it. He told him to make the Ark out of gopherwood and to cover the inside and outside with a substance called pitch, which would preserve the wood and make it waterproof. He also gave Noah precise measurements of how long, wide, and tall to build the Ark. God also gave Noah directions about who would be on the Ark once it was time to board. He told Noah to save his entire family as well as two of every (seven pairs of some) land-dwelling, air-breathing animal. This meant two of every mammal, bird, reptile, and amphibian—all of them would be on the Ark together and together they would all be saved.

Noah built the Ark to provide a way of salvation. He and his family went through the door of the Ark to be saved. But the Ark was also a warning to all those living on earth of a coming judgment—a judgment on all who had rejected God.

Right before the rains of the Flood began to fall, God called out to Noah and told him to enter the Ark. God also brought the animals to Noah to go

The descendants of Noah's family would create many ancient civilizations. From the Tower of Babel, to Egypt, China, Greece, and India, you can trace the history of these and other countries and empires back to the sons and grandsons of Noah.

Just as Noah's family would be the source of future human generations, the animals on the Ark would help replenish each animal kind after the Flood.

on board. Noah and his family had to go through a door into the Ark to be saved, and God shut the door behind them (Genesis 7:16). By putting Noah and his family on the Ark, God preserved humanity. Only eight people from the entire human race were saved on Noah's Ark. We can call these people the "Rescued Race."

We are all members of the "fallen race" and have to go through a "door" to be saved so that we won't be separated from God forever. Just as Noah had to have faith to build the Ark and receive salvation, we also have to have faith to be saved. The Son of God, Jesus, came to earth as the babe in a manger, to pay the price for our sin. Jesus said, "I am the door. If anyone enters by me, he will be saved, and will go in and out and find pasture" (John 10:9). After Noah entered the Ark, God Himself closed the door. Those people outside who did not enter the Ark's door were left to face the terrible judgment of the Flood. In the same way God saved Noah through the Ark, the Lord Jesus Christ is our Ark of salvation. That's the most important thing we all need to understand.

The Ark had only one door which Noah and his family had to go through to be saved from the Flood. In the same way, there is only one door for us to go through to be saved from what our sin did to us—that door is Jesus (John 10:9). We go through that door when we receive by faith what Jesus did on the Cross for us by dying and then being raised from the dead. We have only

this one life on earth to make sure we enter Christ's door of salvation. Make sure you do! We will learn more about this when we discuss the "saved race."

God was with Noah and his family throughout their frightening year on the Ark. During that time, He specially made sure they were safe. When we receive Jesus as our Savior, God tells us that we will live forever with Him after we die. And no one can take that away from us.

God's Son, the Lord Jesus Christ, is like Noah's Ark. Jesus came to save the human race. Just as Noah and his family were saved by the Ark, rescued by God from the floodwaters, so anyone who believes in Jesus as Lord and Savior will be rescued by God from the final judgment which the Bible tells us will be by fire that will destroy the earth (and the whole universe) (2 Peter 3:7). The "Rescued Race" reminds us that God has made sure we have an Ark of salvation just as He did for Noah.

But because even this "Rescued Race" were also members of the "Fallen Race," it didn't take long for humanity to again rebel against God and His Word. About 100 years after the Flood, God again judged the wickedness of man. This time the judgment resulted in a "Divided Race."

Related Scripture List:
Genesis 6:5-8
Genesis 7:16
John 10:9
Hebrews 11:7
2 Peter 3:7

Timeline	Description	Bible Verse
0	The fountains of the great deep broke apart, and the windows of heaven were opened; it began to rain. This happened on the seventeenth day of the second month. Noah actually entered the Ark seven days before this.	Genesis 7:11
40	Rain fell for 40 days, and then water covered the earth's highest places (at that time) by over ~20 feet (15 cubits) and began the stage of flooding until the next milestone.	Genesis 7:11–12
150	The water rose to its highest level (covering the whole earth) sometime between the 40th and 150th day, and the end of these 150 days was the seventeenth day of the seventh month. The Ark rested on the mountains of Ararat. On the 150th day, the springs of the great deep were shut off, and the rain from above ceased, and the water began continually receding.	Genesis 7:24–8:5
150 + 74 = 224	The tops of the mountains became visible on the tenth month, first day.	Genesis 8:5
224 + 40 = 264	After 40 more days, Noah sent out a raven.	Genesis 8:6
264 + 7 = 271	The dove was sent out seven days after the raven. It had no resting place and returned to Noah.	Genesis 8:8–12
271 + 7 = 278	After seven more days, Noah sent out the dove again. It returned again but this time with an olive leaf in its beak.	Genesis 8:10–11
278 + 7 = 285	After seven more days, Noah sent out the dove again, and it did not return.	Genesis 8:12
314	Noah removed the cover of the Ark on the first day of the first month. The surface of the earth was dried up, and Noah could verify this to the extent of what he could see.	Genesis 8:13
370 (371 if counting the first day and last day as full days)	The earth was dry, and God commanded Noah's family and the animals to come out of the Ark. From the first day of the year during the daylight portion, there were 29.5 more days left in the month plus 26.5 more days left in the second month until the exit.	Genesis 8:14–17, Genesis 7:11

* This table uses a 360-day calendar that many ancient people groups used and was even utilized in the Bible in places.[9]

When we look at our world today, there is evidence everywhere for Noah's Flood. When God sent the Flood as judgment for the wickedness of mankind, it affected everything—even the shapes of the continents. Originally, the created world was one large landmass—but the impact of the global Flood resulted in the continents we see today and wiped away most other clues about Noah's world before the Flood. What do we really know about the pre-Flood world?

→ People were skilled at music and crafting things of bronze and iron (Gen. 4:20-22).

→ Noah also had the skills to accomplish the construction of the Ark on the scale needed.

→ There was a variety of animal kinds.

→ There was a garden to the east in Eden.

→ A river in Eden divided into multiple rivers (The Garden and these rivers were destroyed during the Flood even though the name Euphrates is used for the name of a river in today's post-Flood world).[10]

Pishon, which flowed around the whole land of Havilah where gold is—the gold was good, and also bdellium and onyx were found there.

Gihon—flowed around the whole land of Cush.

Tigris—flows east of Assyria.

And the fourth river is the Euphrates (Genesis 2:8–14).

SCIENCE→ Wait…what about all those fossils?

Remember when we talked about the fallen race? We mentioned that if the Creation was "very good" as God tells us it was after He created all things, then how can fossils of dead animals showing evidence of diseases exist? Well, they had to come after what we call the "Fall"—after Adam sinned.

A fossil is some sort of trace of anything that was once living, that has been preserved in some way such as remains or impressions, mostly in sedimentary rock all over the earth.

We can learn a lot about life from the past because we find these fossils of them (or parts of them). There have been fossil finds of plants, animals in many stages of their life, insects, and "snapshots" in time like a fish eating another fish and even a sea reptile giving birth.

Fossil tree shown in several rock layers

→ Fossils need certain conditions to form. Fossils don't take long to form—they just require the right conditions (quick burial by water and lots of mud)!

→ Fossils can be formed quickly. In Kentucky, trees are often found with their base in one rock layer and their tops in another rock layer, sometimes in a layer of coal. And in California, a fossil of a whale was found that went through many rock layers. If rock layers take millions of years to form, the trees and the whale would have decayed and been long gone by the time the next rock layer formed.

→ Fossils around the world are evidence of a worldwide flood, not millions of years. We find fossils of sea creatures in rock layers that cover all the continents. For example, most of the rock layers in the walls of the Grand Canyon (more than a mile above sea level) contain marine fossils. Fossilized shellfish are even found in the Himalayan Mountains.[11]

SCIENCE→ Why aren't fossils from humans found?

First of all, God sent the Flood to "blot out man whom I have created" (Genesis 6:7), which basically means to obliterate the population and all the evil they had done (except for Noah and his family). This means the Flood would cause utter destruction to what man had been involved in.

Second, creation scientists believe most of the original continents were subducted into the mantle as part of what happened during the Flood, and mostly new material built the continents we now have. This means most of what was on the land would have been totally destroyed.

Third, most of the fossil record is of marine snails, corals, plants and insects. In Flood rocks, very few land animals are found as whole skeletons, so it would be very unlikely to find remains of humans.[12]

After the Great Flood, Noah and his descendants began life anew. With a fresh start, God gave Noah and his family directions to spread out over the earth and repopulate the earth. While this command may seem simple, man fell short of fulfilling God's commandment once again as the effects of sin resulting in man's wickedness took hold. Chapter 11 of Genesis describes the rebellion that happened only about 100 years after the great Flood. This rebellion occurred at a place called the Tower of Babel. Instead of spreading over the earth as God told them, the people stayed together and built a giant tower that reached far into the heavens. We can't say for sure, but I believe they were probably worshiping the heavens instead of the God who made the heavens. Certainly, they did not obey God's simple command. Because man had once again disobeyed, God judged the people by confusing their languages. At this point in history, the Bible tells us that man had only one language. It must have been terrifying for these people when all of a sudden, they tried to communicate with one another and they couldn't. People they may have known their whole lives were suddenly cut off from them. From what we understand from Genesis 10, God must have given each family group a different language. This made it impossible for the groups to understand each other, forcing them to split apart and find different places to live. Because of God's judgment, people spread over the earth just as God had told them to do in the first place.

Because of the new language each group had, and because of mountains, rivers, and oceans, people from different family groups couldn't mix together easily. As a result, people groups with all sorts of customs formed. Also, differences in the human body like skin shade, eye shape, hair color, and so on became more and more obvious as new groups of children were born. This resulted in the special differences within the human race that we see today. Now I know what you might be thinking… this may sound like evolution. But

#set the
TONE

The Tower of Babel was the start of the many cultures we see today.

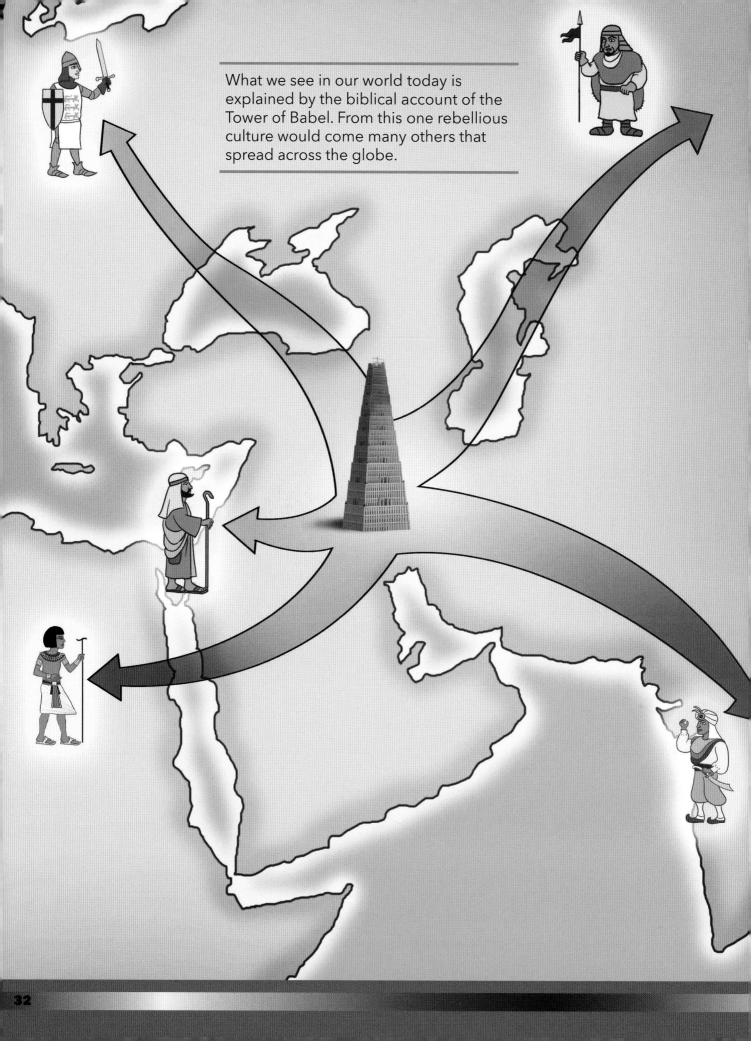

What we see in our world today is explained by the biblical account of the Tower of Babel. From this one rebellious culture would come many others that spread across the globe.

the truth is, these changes have nothing to do with evolution. When God created Adam and Eve, He gave the human race lots of ability for variation that would show up as people spread over the earth.

Charles Darwin's ideas on evolution originally divided people into races. Did you know that the Bible does not even use the word *race* when talking about people? The Bible simply describes all human beings as being of "one blood" or from "one man" (Acts 17:26). We are all related. All humans come from the first man, Adam, who was created in the image of God. The Last Adam, Jesus Christ, also became a member of Adam's family when He was born to Mary. Any of Adam's family can be saved because God's Son became our relative when he became the God-man. He came to earth and became like one of us so He could die for our sins. That is why the message of Jesus and salvation should be preached to everyone all over the world.

Now let's talk about the topic of the skin color to help us understand what happened because of the Tower of Babel.

It's important to understand that every human has the same basic skin color. Any difference in that color is simply a matter of the shade of our skin—how light or dark we are. Imagine going with someone to a store to choose a paint color for your house. Let's say you want to paint the house brown. You pick out a really light brown, a darker brown, and a really dark brown. It's sort of like that with people.

There are no truly "black" or "white" people. All humans are actually shades of brown because of the pigment in our skin. This pigment is what changes the shade of this one main color. Now this pigment has a special name. It's called melanin. It is pronounced "mel-uh-nin." Melanin is actually a brown color.

In truth, it's not what "color" someone is, but what shade of the color they are! In fact, all humans technically have color in their skin—unless someone is an albino and they don't have any of the pigment melanin because of a problem in their genes. Such a situation can cause terrible problems because we need melanin for our skin and our eyes to be healthy—and it helps our body in other ways too.

So, let's review. We know that Adam and Eve were the first two people. Their children had children and so on, and they filled the earth before the Flood. However, the number of people in the whole world was only eight during the Flood of Noah—the eight people in Noah's family who were saved on the Ark. From Noah's three sons and their wives have come all the people groups and nations of the world.

#set the
TONE

There are no "races"—only the human race.

Cultures may vary greatly, but many of these people groups around the world have Creation and global Flood legends in common, including details from biblical history.

We think the skin shade of Noah and his family was a mixture of light, middle, and dark brown because of the genes in their DNA. God most likely made Adam and Eve with a mixture of genes for skin shade. He created them like this so their children could be diverse, unique, and all different shades of brown. Noah and his wife's skin may have been a middle shade of brown. Because of the way the genetic code works, if they were middle brown their sons and wives could have children with lots of different shades of brown. Remember, before the Tower of Babel there was only one language, and everybody lived in the same area. During this time, people from different families could easily marry each other. This probably meant most people's skin was not very dark or very light (like we see in the contrast of the people of today), but more a brown shade in the middle.

Because of what happened at the Tower of Babel, as families moved away from each other, some people ended up with dark brown skin while others ended up with light brown skin. The resulting difference in skin color simply depended on who people married and their unique genetic code. But skin shade was not the only physical attribute that began to change in the people. As families moved, people groups ended up with differences in skin shade, eye shape, eye color, height, and lots of other characteristics as well.

The Bible has been telling us all along. All people come from the first two humans, Adam and Eve. Scientists who study our human bodies have discovered that all people belong to one race. Scientists "discovered" this fact back in the year 2000, and the headline was so startling that it made

international news. These scientists didn't start with a biblical worldview; perhaps they should have just opened a Bible—and they would have known the truth much sooner.

Sadly, because of the false teaching of evolution, many people thought humans belonged to different races. A lot of people even believed (because of Darwin's false evolutionary ideas) that some humans are more closely related to apes than others. But this is not true! Apes are animals, and humans are not related to animals. Humans were created in God's image. Animals are not. Humans are all related to each other—we are all one race. We are one family, one blood. Yes, there are different people groups all over the earth, but we are all members of Adam's family. Take a moment to think about this simple truth. Everyone is our relative. All humans belong to one big family. That's why it's important to understand that we are all equal because God created us. Because we are all related, we are all sinners, and we all need to receive the free gift of salvation Jesus offers us. We should never look down on someone because they have a different skin shade or eye shape than us. Color and shape are such small details. While they may make us look a certain way, they do not define who we truly are.

I come from Australia where there is a people group with a darker shade of skin called the Australian Aboriginal people. Because of the false teaching of evolution, some people considered the Australian Aboriginal people to be closely related to apes like gorillas and chimps. They even thought that the Aboriginal people were a different race of people altogether. Because of this, the Aboriginal people were considered to be a lower race. People treated them terribly just because scientists who believe "evolution" said they were more closely related to animals. But the truth is the Bible tells us we are all equal. The Christian missionaries who came to Australia teaching God's Word knew the Aboriginal people were members of the human family and were children of Adam and Eve just like all of us. That's why they took the message of Jesus and salvation all the way to Australia, and we should do the same for every people group on this earth.

So rather than talking about races, we should talk about people groups or ethnic groups when we think of the variety of people made in the image of God. We are all one race, just divided into different groups, each with their own way of building things, making food, and even dressing. Jesus died for people of every nation, tribe, language, and people group (Revelation 14:6).

Now, if all humans belong to one race, then really, there is no such thing as what some call "interracial" marriage (for example, when a "black" person marries a "white" person). However, the Bible explains there are actually two very different "races" of people that should never marry each other. These are what I call the "spiritual races." There are only two types of "spiritual races." Those who are Christians and those who are not. Someone from the saved race should never knowingly marry someone from the unsaved race. This is a reminder that the Created Race, Adam's race, has a spiritual problem called sin. That's why God sent His Son to be our Savior. And when Christians get married, they need to make sure who they are marrying is a Christian too (2 Corinthians 6:14).

The Bible gives us a glimpse into God's view of marriage between people from different groups in the accounts of Rahab and Ruth.

CULTURE → "Interracial" Marriage

It's hard to imagine that there were once laws against different so-called "races" marrying each other, but there were. Before and after the Civil War, a number of laws were put in place that made what was called "interracial" marriage against the law. It was only in 1967 that such marriages became legal throughout the United States. Mildred and Richard Loving brought the landmark case to the U.S. Supreme Court after being sentenced to one year in jail for marrying.[13] But there's no such thing as "'interracial" marriage biologically because all humans belong to the same one race.[14] If people had believed the Bible's true account of history, such wrong laws would not have been enacted.

Culture is defined in the secular world as "the customary beliefs, social forms, and material traits of a [so-called] racial, religious, or social group; also: the characteristic features of everyday existence (such as diversions or a way of life) shared by people in a place or time." [15]

The biblical account of the Flood of Noah and the Tower of Babel explains what we see in our world today—many different, yet all uniquely beautiful, cultures scattered across the globe. As the descendants of Noah's family grew in number, they didn't want to do what God said to do. Interesting, isn't it? Even after the Flood, people still continued to disobey God.

When God changed the languages of the families at Babel, the people were forced to abandon the project and they scattered throughout the world. They developed unique cultures, languages, and traditions, but still remained the human race. In the past, many cultures either met in trade or war. Some were overtaken or destroyed by larger empires. Today, modern technology enables us to go anywhere in the world or communicate with others. This also makes it easy to share God's Word and the gospel with people all over the world!

#set the
TONE

There is a lot of variety among the people groups of the world today—but all can trace their heritage back to the Garden of Eden.

#set the
TONE

Around 7% of
skin cells are
melanocytes,
and produce
melanin.

In the Book of Joshua, chapter 2, we learn of a Canaanite named Rahab. The Canaanites were an evil culture and were related to a man named Canaan, the son of Ham (who was a son of Noah). The Bible tells us that Canaan was cursed. The Canaanites were so bad that the Israelites were told not to marry these evil people. But Rahab married an Israelite (Matthew 1:5). The reason she was allowed to do so was because she stopped being like the evil people in her family and trusted in the true God like the Israelites. Rahab chose to change her spiritual race. Once she put her trust in the true Creator God, she could marry a man from God's people regardless of what people group she came from.

The same can be said of Ruth, who was a Moabite. Ruth also married an Israelite. Before her marriage, she changed her spiritual race by putting her faith in the one true God (Ruth 1:16).

When Rahab and Ruth became children of God, there was no longer any reason they couldn't marry Israelites who trusted in God. Even though they were originally from different people groups, by putting their faith in God, they joined the "Saved Race."

If someone wants to use the word "interracial," then the only "interracial" marriage that God says we should never enter into is when a Christian (a child of the Last Adam, Jesus) marries one who has not received the free gift of salvation. The Bible calls a person who has not received the gift of salvation someone who is "dead" in their sins. Later on, we will learn about this "Lost Race."

Even though the human race was divided at the Tower of Babel, God fulfilled His promise of a Savior. He made sure a member of Adam's race would come to pay the penalty for our sin, so we could be saved (the word "redeemed" means saved) and live with God forever.

Through the rebellion, the language confusion, and even the divided world, God was working to redeem a people who would become part of His godly "race." The Bible clearly says in Galatians 3:28, Colossians 3:11, and Romans 10:12–13 that there is no distinction between male or female or Jew or Greek when it comes to salvation. When we trust in Christ, we are no longer divided. As Christians, we are one in Christ and have a common purpose—to live for Him who made us. All humans belong to the "Created Race" and the "Fallen Race." We all need the message of salvation to be a part of the "Saved Race." However, not all people will receive the free gift of salvation, and so they will remain members of the "Lost Race."

This brings us to the most important message of the Bible—an understanding of the "Saved Race."

Related Scripture List:
Genesis 11
Ruth 1:16
Acts 17:26
Romans 10:12–13
2 Corinthians 6:14
Galatians 3:28
Colossians 3:11
Revelation 14:6

SCIENCE → Understanding the UV Factor

We mentioned earlier that the amount of sunlight where you live can make a difference in your skin tone (if you're exposed to it a lot) up to a maximum determined by your genes. Sunlight contains ultraviolet or UV rays. This can help trigger increased melanin in your skin, but too much sun can lead to cancer. While melanin protects us from the harmful effects of too many UV rays, it doesn't determine our basic skin tones. Genetics do that—though people groups with more exposure to the sun will usually produce more melanin in their skin and be darker in skin tone. However, this is not always the case—for example, the Inuit people group live in the North, yet still have dark skin tones.

If you live in certain regions of the world, you may have more or less exposure to sunlight. Here is a skin tone map. Notice that skin shades tend to be darker in areas where UV rays are more intense, like near the equator.[16]

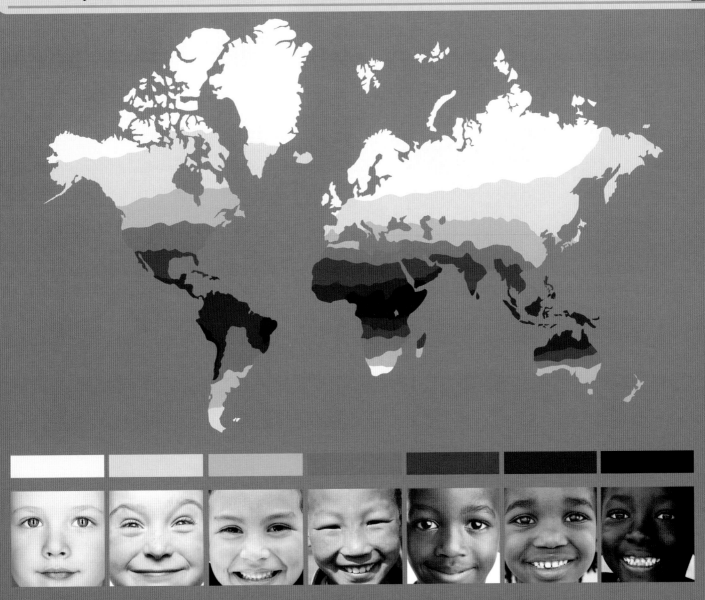

Cultures and Conflict

One definition of "race" is "a category of humankind that shares certain distinctive physical traits."[17] While racism is hatred or discrimination often focused on the physical differences among people, ethnicity focuses on something else.

People are often categorized as different ethnicities—which simply means they "belong to a social group with a common national or cultural tradition."[18] In the past century, there have been numerous examples of terrible violence among different ethnic groups in some places—and as a result "ethnic cleansing," the mass murder or expulsion of some people groups have taken place.

Choosing to Co-exist

Sometimes people choose to move to other places, taking their unique cultures with them. It's a wonderful opportunity for the new arrivals and their new neighbors to learn about the others' culture—its foods, holidays, history, and more. Remember, no matter what someone's ethnicity, or culture, they are always part of just one race—the human race!

Testing Your Ancestry

Genealogy is the study of your family history. It's popular to do DNA testing these days. It can be used to solve crimes, or more commonly, to determine your history and family connections. This simply means you can take a test using saliva or blood, and science can tell you a lot about your health, genetics, and family's geographical history. You can also find distant relatives on genealogy sites through the testing.

We all tend to identify with a people group—usually from information passed down to us from historical family documents or oral history from past or present generations of family members. Genealogy testing can often surprise people by showing genetic connections to other people groups or places of which they were unaware.

These tests show we aren't defined by where we live now—our bodies reveal a genetic history that is rich and diverse. Cultures, nationalities, or other social, religious, or political categories do not mean there is more than one human race. In our many differences, we remain one blood—one race—but with great diversity within the one human race.

A History of Slavery and the Bible[19]

Some of the earliest civilizations that we have found evidence of practiced various forms of slavery. When slavery is cruelly forced on someone, it is shameful, and it has continued throughout history. Sadly, did you know that slavery in various forms still exists in our world today?

What does the Bible say about Slavery?

As with many things, those who have supported cruel slavery and those who fought against it often used the Bible as a way to justify, or try to prove, their arguments. Two kinds of slavery are described in the Bible. One is like a servant who was paid a wage. The other is a person forced to work without being paid. Which types of "slavery" did the Bible condemn?

→ Slaves under the laws Moses wrote in the first five books of the Bible were different from the harshly treated slaves of other societies; they were more like paid servants.

→ The slaves (called bondservants) who are described this way in the Bible were people who worked for a time to pay off debts and could earn their freedom. The Bible condemns those who steal, buy, and sell people as property (1 Timothy 1:10).

→ Israelites could sell themselves as slaves/bondservants to have their debts covered, make a wage, have housing, and be set free after six years. Foreigners could sell themselves as slaves/bondservants as well.

→ The Bible addressed slavery as a reality in a sin-cursed world and didn't ignore it, but instead gave rules for good treatment by both masters and servants and revealed they are equal under Christ.

#set the
TONE

Biblical Christians still lead the fight to end slavery in modern times.

The use of the term "one blood" in Acts 17:26 is very significant. If "races" were really of different "bloods," then we could not all be saved by the shedding of the blood of one Savior. It is because the entire human race can be seen to come from one man—Adam (and one woman, Eve)—that we know we can trust in one Savior, Jesus Christ (the "Last Adam").

Christians opposed slavery because it was seen to be contrary to the value that God places on every human being, and the fact that God "has made from one blood every nation of men to dwell on all the face of the earth" (Acts 17:26, NKJV). The last letter that the revival evangelist John Wesley ever wrote was to William Wilberforce, encouraging Wilberforce in his fight to see slavery ended.

He wrote:

'Reading this morning a tract wrote by a poor African, I was particularly struck by that circumstance that a man who has a black skin, being wronged or outraged by a white man, can have no redress; it being a "law" in our colonies that the oath of a black against a white goes for nothing. What villainy is this?'

Wesley concentrated on the value of a person, no matter the color (actually shade) of his or her skin. It is this principle of the value God places on human beings—a biblical principle—which was Wesley's motivation in opposing slavery.

The famous hymn writer John Newton at one time actually captained slave ships. He did so even after he became a Christian because he was influenced by the prevailing attitudes of "race" in his society; it took time for him to realize his errors. But when he did—he spent the last part of his life campaigning against slavery. He wrote movingly and disturbingly of the suffering of slaves in the ships' galleys in his small book *Thoughts upon the African Slave Trade*.

Some "white" Christians have assumed that the so-called "curse of Ham" (Genesis 9:25) was to cause Ham's descendants to be "black" and to be cursed. While it is likely that most African peoples are descended from Ham (Cush, Phut, and Mizraim—three of Noah's grandsons), it is not likely that they are the descendants of Canaan, who settled further north; the curse was actually declared on Canaan, not Ham!

However, there is no evidence from Genesis that the curse had anything to do with skin shade. Others have suggested that the "mark of Cain" in Genesis 4 was that he was turned dark-skinned. Again, there is absolutely no evidence of this in Scripture, and in any case, Cain's descendants were more or less wiped out in the Flood.

By the way, the use of this lie to attempt to justify some sort of evil associated with dark skin is based on an assumption that the other people descended from Noah's sons were all light-skinned, like "white" people today. That assumption can also not be found in Scripture and is very unlikely to be true.

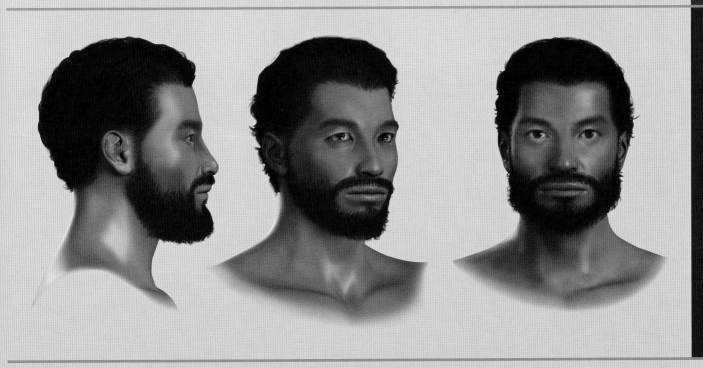

The issue of racism is just one of many reasons why Answers in Genesis opposes evolution. Darwinian evolution can easily be used to suggest that some "races" are more evolved than others; that is, the common belief is that "blacks" are less evolved. Biblical Christianity cannot be used that way—unless it is twisted by people who have deliberately misunderstood what the Bible actually teaches. On top of this, rejecting the Bible, a book that is not racist, because one may think evolution is superior is a sad alternative. Recall Darwin's prediction of non-white "races":

> 'At some future period, not very distant as measured by centuries, the civilized races of man will almost certainly exterminate and replace the savage races throughout the world.' [23]

Basically, Darwin saw a future where more "advanced races" would completely destroy "less advanced races." While Darwin's ideas did not create racism, it was used to justify the racism that already may have existed in a person's heart.[24]

Evolution is the idea that life began from a single cell and, over a long, long time, developed into all the plants, animals, and people we see today.

Saved
RACE

In Genesis 3:15, right after the first sin, God said there would be hatred between Eve and her descendants and the serpent (Satan) and his descendants. The verse actually says that the serpent (the devil) will bruise a man's heel and that a man will bruise the serpent's head. Now, it may not seem to make a lot of sense, but this verse really sums up the message of the entire Bible. This verse provides hope to Adam, Eve, and all of us because it is actually giving the message that we can be saved and become members of the saved race.

The "head" and the "heel" of Genesis 3:15 may seem like a great mystery, but it's all about the battle between the devil and Jesus—and, of course, Jesus won the battle!

But what does this mean? Genesis 22:18 gives us more understanding about who the promised "Seed" (or Offspring) of the woman is who will bruise the head of the serpent. This verse says that Abraham, one of Eve's descendants, would be father to a "Seed" who will bless everyone. Later in Galatians 3:16, Paul also speaks about the blessings of this "Seed" and the promises that were made and fulfilled through Him.

So, who is this "Seed"? The "Seed" is Jesus (God's Son who stepped into history to be Jesus Christ, the God-man, when He became the babe in a manger).

The phrase "her Seed" in Genesis 3:15 is actually a prophecy about the One who would be the baby who was born in Bethlehem; this was the birth of the Last Adam, Jesus Christ, over 2,000 years ago.

God's Word tells us that the Creator God became a man so that as a perfect man, He could pay the price of our sin by dying on the Cross. When Jesus was on the cross, He suffered and died. This is what it means when Genesis 3:15 says the serpent will "bruise his heel."

#set the
TONE

John 3:16:
"For God so loved the world, that he gave his only Son, that whoever believes in him should not perish but have eternal life."

#set the TONE

With Jesus' death and resurrection, He paid the price for our sin and offers the chance to be saved.

But because He is the eternal Creator, Jesus is all-powerful. So after He was buried He rose from the dead, overcoming death. The one who has power over death has never-ending power. "Bruising the serpent's head" is the wound Satan received through Christ's victory over him on the Cross. He is a defeated enemy. The devil still roams the earth hurting humanity and seeking destruction, but he can never win the war against God, and one day God will put him away forever.

Jesus' whole mission was to take away sin and overcome death. Remember what we talked about in chapter two when we discussed the first blood sacrifice of the animals? God showed us the sacrifice that needed to happen when He made clothes for Adam and Eve out of animal skins.

God killed at least one animal to provide the animal skins as a covering for their sin. This was the origin of clothing for humans. It was also a picture of Jesus, who is the "Lamb of God, who takes away the sin of the world" (John 1:29). The covering from skins God provided for Adam and Eve couldn't take away their sin. But it was a picture of what happened when Jesus died and rose again.

We could never live with our holy God as sinners. But because of what Jesus did on the Cross, if we receive God's free gift of salvation, we can stand before a holy God one day and live with Him forever. We can't get to heaven by just being kind or by doing nice deeds for others. Adam and Eve knew they had sinned, so they tried to hide that sin by making clothes out of fig leaves. But we can't pay for our sin—only a perfect man could do that. This is why God sent His Son to be that perfect man.

Now, if it is only God who is able to take away our sin, how can we make sure He has truly taken it away? The Bible makes it very clear in Romans 10:9 by saying that if we confess our sin to God and believe in His Son, then we will be saved.

This is how we become part of the "saved race." First, we tell God that we know we are sinners and that we are sorry for choosing to sin (this is called repentance). We also tell Jesus we know that He died and rose from the dead to take away our sins. It's as simple as that. We then receive the free gift of salvation from our Creator, and we get to spend forever with Him as members of the "Saved Race."

The first Adam, our great great (and many more greats) grandfather 6,000 years ago, was judged by God because of his sin. He eventually died, and his body turned to dust. Because of his sin, death came upon all of Adam's race, which means all of us.

Related Scripture List:
Genesis 3:15
Genesis 22:18
John 1:29
Romans 10:9
Galatians 3:16
Hebrews 2:14

The Last Adam, Jesus Christ, also had to experience the judgment of God—not for His sins, because He lived a perfect life, but for the sins of humans around the globe. He died on the Cross to pay for our sin. But He did not stay dead, and His body did not decay. On the third day after His death, He rose again, and so won the war with the devil. He overcame the power of death for all people who believe in Him (Hebrews 2:14). This is the message of the babe born in Bethlehem that we should celebrate every day, but we especially do so at Christmas. It starts with the creation of a perfect world, and then, because of our sin, leads to our need for a Savior—which is why Jesus stepped into history to become the perfect God-man 2,000 years ago. Because of what Jesus did, we can become members of the "Saved Race." But those who do not receive this free gift of salvation will remain members of the "Lost Race." These people are spiritually dead, and it's an important "race" we need to understand.

#set the
TONE

Anyone anywhere in the world can become part of the Saved Race.

Where Science Went Wrong

Johann Blumenbach

For a period of time in history in the 1700s and 1800s, "race science" was the focus of many different kinds of scientists all around the world. Having embraced the concept of evolution, even of humans, they began to make assumptions about people who lived in what they considered were less advanced cultures compared to their own at the time. At the heart of this study was the mistaken idea that some "races" were more evolved, and therefore better, than other "races." German scientist Johann Friedrich Blumenbach is credited with assigning humans into five "race" categories in the late 1700s:[25]

→ Caucasian or white race (example: Europeans)

→ Mongolian or yellow race (example: East and Central Asians)

→ Malayan or brown race (example: Southeast Asian and Pacific Islanders)

→ Ethiopian or black race (example: Sub-saharan Africans)

→ American or red race (example: American Indians)

Blumenbach did not necessarily see any difference in the abilities of each "race." Since he felt that the differences among the "races" he assigned were because of their diet, geography, and other external factors, he thought they had originally been Caucasian, and environmental factors caused the differences in their skin color (shade). Therefore, if they were placed in areas away from these factors, he thought these groups would eventually go back to their original 'Caucasian' form.[26]

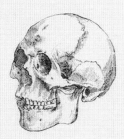 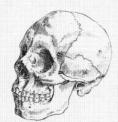 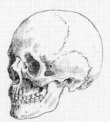 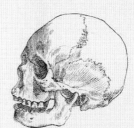 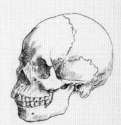

While Blumenbach's theory separated people groups into one of five varieties, based on physical and other differences (for example: the shape of skulls, etc.), he still felt humans were all part of one species.

Scientist Carl Linnaeus who formed the basic classification of plants and animals, also created classifications for humans complete with not just differences in skin shade, but also behavioral traits.

Linnaeus appeared to consider how advanced was the level of cultures as the defining factor for his classifications. But this was incorrect, and bad science based on bias.

SCIENCE → A Terrible Turn—Scientific Racism

However, many other scientists saw only the physical differences among the "races," and they chose instead to focus on an even more fake type of science—racial biology or scientific racism. This science was focused on showing that the "races" were not just different, but different in ways that made the Caucasian race better or more advanced. That suggested the others were not. This led to these groups being ranked in order of more, or less, evolved. These scientists used examples of skull size to determine intelligence, personal preferences of beauty or appearance, and known levels of civilization to make their biased determinations.

Unfortunately, many people listened to these scientists. This awful idea of some races being better than others led to terrible injustices and tragedies for people groups like the Aboriginal people of Australia, Native Americans, and Africans. Many of these people groups were killed to take their land or enslaved and suffered from terrible discrimination and abuse because of this false science-based racism.

A member of the Aboriginal people group in Australia

HISTORY → The Stolen Generations

Before disastrous contact with European explorers, the Aboriginal people of Australia had a diverse mix of both nomadic and permanently settled people groups. These people groups had a wide range of languages and smaller groups or clans within them.

In 1788, the first wave of British colonization began. Epidemics and disease soon almost wiped out the indigenous population. They faced terrible abuses. Their lands and vital water resources were taken and animals traditionally hunted for food were almost destroyed by colonists.

The Aboriginal people were used as forced labor, with no respect to their own culture, languages, or family connections and exploited without payment for their labors. Their children were often removed from the families by the government, placed in schools to be educated outside of their own culture, and trained to be mere servants. This terrible policy is remembered as The Stolen Generations. It is a tragic story that was repeated time and time again throughout the world and history as indigenous people groups were discovered by explorers from more technologically developed nations and those seeking land and resources.

When you pair the terrible idea of "races" of people being at different evolutionary points with the evolutionists' idea of natural selection or survival of the fittest, logically you can theorize that those who are stronger, smarter, more capable are naturally going to dominate and eliminate others weaker and less capable. Now connect that conclusion with the false idea of there being no God and you are not accountable for your actions. You have created a recipe for disaster. You have people who take this false science and use it in terms of horrible political, social, or economic policy.[27]

For example, the Aryan Race was a questionable scientific grouping of people with physical characteristics thought by some to have been European and Western Asian in ancestry. Adolf Hitler's desire to make the so-called Aryan Race pure and supreme led to the murder of millions including Jews, Gypsies, Poles (in Poland), Slavs (in the Ukraine and Russia), specific Christian denominations, and more in extermination camps, medical facilities, and hospitals.

Sadly, other forms of discrimination and racism based on bad science were also rooted in popular ideas of the time such as eugenics, racial sterilization, intelligence testing of immigrants— all based on false ideas of racial superiority or inferiority.[28]

In the mid-20th century most of the scientific community began to turn away from the idea of scientific racism. While there were still a few relating to races and evolution, most began to focus on other directions.

Today, the word "race" isn't even used by a lot of scientists. They use the phrase "continental ancestry" instead, meant to refer to the factors that can be found to link individuals to one or more continents for their historical ancestry. They look at factors like genetics to try to solve these questions of the differences between people groups. Many also see "race" as a social group or construct (idea) rather than a scientific one. The Bible had it right all along and we suggest using the term "people groups."

Auschwitz was the biggest Nazi extermination camp in Europe.

The Bible says in Ephesians 2:1 that anyone who sins is actually dead in their soul. The best way to describe anyone who is not part of the "Saved Race" is that they are dead in their hearts—they are lost from a relationship with their Creator and Savior. They may seem fine on the outside, but as we learned earlier, their sin makes them spiritually lifeless. Sin separates the human race from our holy Creator God. In order to be reunited with Him once again and be a member of the saved race, we must die to our sinful past and be given new life. But the only one who can give us this new life is God through His Son, the Lord Jesus Christ.

So how can someone whose heart is spiritually dead be given new life? God's Word states that anyone who confesses that Jesus Christ is Lord, repents of their sin, and receives Him as their Savior becomes a new creation. Our sin that caused us to be spiritually dead is paid for by what Christ did on the Cross, and we are brought to spiritual life. Through the sacrifice Jesus made on the Cross, we are made new.

But how can this happen?

Almost 2,000 years ago, a Jewish ruler named Nicodemus came to Jesus, curious about who Jesus was and how He was able to perform the miracles and wonders Nicodemus and others had seen (John 3). Jesus then told him an important truth. He told Nicodemus that in order to see the kingdom of God, he must be "born again." After hearing this, Nicodemus was confused. He didn't understand how anyone could be born a second time from their mother. But Jesus wasn't talking about a physical rebirth—He was talking about a spiritual rebirth of the soul.

Jesus explained that we are born once from our mother's womb, but we need to be born again (spiritually) to become a member of the "Saved Race."

#set the
TONE

If you have not received the gift of salvation offered by Jesus, you are part of the lost race.

SCIENCE→ No Longer a Perfect World–Aging Process

When Adam and Eve sinned, all of creation became corrupted. This means that we will be sick sometimes and eventually will die, though we will not enjoy the very long lifespans of people early in

With sin came death—and before death, if you live to be older, comes the process of aging.

Now Nicodemus wondered how in the world a person could be born again when they were already old. Jesus' answer was very clear. Being born again means becoming part of God's family. The word "again" literally means "from above," which in this context means becoming a child of God. This is different than being born like a baby is born. The second birth Jesus is talking about is a spiritual birth. It is something that happens in our heart by the work of the Holy Spirit of God. The Bible tells us that when we are "born again" we are actually made a new creation by God's Holy Spirit.

When I was born again into God's family by the Spirit, my life changed, and my heart changed. From the moment I received Jesus into my life, I knew I was God's child. The things I wanted to do were different. I wanted to learn about God. I learned to trust Jesus and understood that without Him I could never get to heaven. I wanted to go to church and learn more about the Bible. I began to love God more and more. By growing with God, I learned how my sin separated me from Him. Because I was now a part of God's family, I was also more aware of the sin in my life. In my heart I knew I needed Jesus and His forgiveness every day. Being born again means that I can know for sure that I will one day be in heaven with God, my Lord and Savior! When we are born again, we are saved and will live for eternity with the Lord Jesus (John 10:27–30).

And for those who are born twice, the Bible tells us what it will be like as members of the "Saved Race" in Revelation 21:1–4. In this passage John writes

biblical history like Methuselah or Noah. The average life expectancy for humans today is 79 years, though for a few it could reach as high as 120 or slightly over. The process of aging includes:

Signs of Aging Skin
- Dark spots
- Drier skin
- Sagging skin
- Lines or wrinkles

Process of Aging
- Heart rate slows
- High blood pressure
- Bones shrink, weaken
- Less flexibility in muscles
- Balance issues
- Digestive issues
- Lack of bladder control
- Confusion or forgetfulness

about a vision of the future where our sinful world passes away through God's miraculous power, and He creates a new heaven and a new earth. God's new earth will be different than the one we know today, and Scripture even says that this new earth won't have a sea. John also says that in his vision he saw a holy city called "the new Jerusalem." In this city he sees a wedding party with a beautiful bride. There is then a voice heard which proclaims the triumphant news that God's dwelling place is now among His people! For the first time since the days when God dwelt with Adam and Eve in the garden, His presence will once again be with His people! Can you imagine how marvelous this day will be? God will be with us and there will be no more death, no diseases, no more tears, no more pain or mourning—and everyone who is a member of "Saved Race" will live eternally with God forever!

But for those who are not of the "Saved Race," the Bible clearly states they will be members of the "Lost Race." John also tells us in Revelation 20:11–15 that one day there will be a judgment before a great white throne. Everyone who is part of the "Lost Race" will fear the face of the person who sits on this throne. All will stand before God and be judged according to their works, which will be recorded in books. Our works are our actions, our deeds, and our sins. Good deeds are done to honor God, and our sins are anything that does not please God. And our good works can't make us members of the "Saved Race." Even though we may have done good works, even one sin separates us from a perfectly holy God. Anyone who has not trusted in Christ for salvation and

#set the
TONE

Despite attempts by modern science to slow or stop aging, science cannot offer hope for eternal life.

God created the heavens and the earth, the Garden of Eden where Adam sinned, and also sent His son, Jesus, to die on the Cross for our sins. From Creation to the Cross, God had a plan to provide salvation from our sin.

Related Scripture List:
John 3
John 10:27-30
Ephesians 2:1
Revelation 21:1-4
Revelation 20:11-15
Revelation 21:5-8

whose name is not written in the Book of Life will be cast into the lake of fire and die a second death—which means to be eternally separated from God (Revelation 21:5–8).

For those who are only born once, they will sadly die twice. Their bodies will die and return to dust. But that's not where it ends. Their souls, the eternal part of a person, will die a different sort of death forever. Because they are separated from God and punished for their sinful actions, they will not be able to live with God when they are resurrected and will have to be in a place the Bible calls hell. They then will have this "second death" as part of the "Lost Race." I plead with all reading this: don't be a member of the "Lost Race."

But for those who are born twice, when their bodies die, their soul, the eternal part of a person, will then be with the Lord and spend forever in a place the Bible calls the new heavens and earth (heaven). They will also be resurrected with a body, just like the Lord Jesus was after His death on the Cross. They will be members of the "Lamb's Race" for eternity. I pray every one of you reading this book will be with me in heaven forever and ever as we live with the "Lamb," the Lord Jesus Christ, for ever and ever.

In John 1:29, John the Baptist saw Jesus coming toward him one day as he was preaching by a river. At that moment when John saw Jesus, he stopped preaching and told all those listening, "Behold, the Lamb of God, who takes away the sin of the world!"

What would the people in John's day have thought of when he said this? They would have thought about their animal sacrifices. Remember the first blood sacrifice we talked about after Adam and Eve sinned in the garden of Eden? This was the first blood sacrifice and the origin of clothing, as a covering for sin. Later, God gave instructions to Moses on how to offer sacrifices in the temple to cover the sins of the people. These sacrifices that brought the death of animals served as a reminder of how serious sin is, how holy God is, and that sin must be paid for. However, these animal sacrifices had to be made over and over again, as they could not ultimately take sin away. Only God's Son can permanently remove sin. Jesus did this by becoming a perfect man (He never sinned, not even once) and then becoming the sacrifice for our sin by dying on the Cross. The animal sacrifices were also a picture of what was to come in Jesus Christ, "the Lamb of God, who takes away the sin of the world."

These animal sacrifices were pointing to the fact that, in time, God would provide the perfect sacrifice who would pay the penalty for our sin—the Lord Jesus Christ.

Also, God's special people, the Israelites, would have thought about an event called the Exodus. The Exodus was what happened when God's people were taken out of slavery in Egypt, leading up to the miracle of the crossing of the Red Sea. Exodus 12:21–27 tells us that Moses called for all the elders and told them to pick out a lamb and to kill this Passover lamb. They were then instructed to take a branch of hyssop (a wild shrub), dip it into the blood of the lamb, and paint the doorframe with the blood. He then told the Israelites that they should not go outside of the door until morning. All of this was done

#set the
TONE

John the Baptist referred to Jesus as "the Lamb of God, who takes away the sin of the world!"

Jesus was born to sacrifice Himself on a cross for our salvation, and the account of His extraordinary life is found in God's Word, the Holy Bible.

because the Lord was going to pass through and strike down the firstborn male in any household who did not have the blood on their doorposts. This was how God "passed over" the houses covered by the blood. This action is still celebrated today as Passover, when God delivered the Israelites from slavery and saved His people. It was a reminder of the need for a sacrifice for sin, but also a reminder that one day God would send the ultimate sacrifice, the Lord Jesus Christ.

We read that God's Son became a man (the God-man Jesus), and He died and rose again. Because of this powerful sacrifice, we don't offer animal sacrifices anymore. Because of Jesus being the sacrifice for our sin, those who receive the free gift of salvation will spend forever with Jesus, the Lamb. And when we receive this gift, we are born into His family! It is called being "born again." Just as the Lord passed over the houses marked with blood, those who have been saved by the blood of the Lamb of God will not face the second death on Judgment Day.

One day, God will judge this earth and universe by fire and make a new heaven and earth. Remember the verse we read in the "Lost Race" in Revelation 21:1–4 when John saw the holy city of New Jerusalem? We're told something very special about this holy city. Revelation 21:22–27 tells us that in the new place there is no need for the light of the sun or moon—the glory of God gives light to everything. The Scripture actually says, "The Lamb is its light." It also says that all who are saved (anyone whose name was written in the Lamb's Book of Life) walk in this light and that there is never any darkness. Those who are born again will dwell with Jesus the Lamb—we will be members of the "Lamb's Race." Wow! What a wonderful future this will be.

But, how sad for those who will not be members of the "Lamb's Race." Revelation 21:5–8 tells us that on this day the one who sits on the throne will say, "Behold, I make all things new." God is the Alpha and the Omega—the beginning and the end—and He gives eternal life freely to all. God invites us

into His family to live forever with Him. However, God makes it very clear that we must be without sin to enter into His family. All sin separates us from God, and there is only one way to remove that sin—through receiving the forgiveness offered through Jesus.

Yes, all humans are members of the "Created Race" made in the image of God, the "Fallen Race" having a sinful nature from Adam, and the "Divided Race" of all kinds of ethnic groups. But it's so very important that we also become members of the "Rescued Race" given grace by God, the "Saved Race" saved from God's judgment, and the "Lamb's Race" covered by Jesus' blood. Please don't remain a member of the "Lost Race" under judgment for your sin.

The good news is that God has provided a way back to Him, so we don't have to remain a member of the "Lost Race."

"For God so loved the world that He gave His only begotten Son, that whoever believes in Him should not perish, but have everlasting life" (John 3:16).

Jesus Christ lived totally without sin and suffered on behalf of the human race. He did all of this to pay the price for sin so we wouldn't have to be separated from God forever. We need Jesus because our holy God had to have the price of our sin paid for to satisfy justice. Jesus was the perfect sacrifice. He died on a Cross as a sacrificial lamb. But His life did not end, and on the third day He rose again and overcame death. Now, all who truly believe in Him and those who are sorry for their sin can repent and trust in Him. We can't do anything by ourselves to get to Heaven! Because Jesus became the sacrificial lamb for the sins of the world, everyone who receives the free gift of salvation Jesus provides can come to God and live forever with Him.

What a wonderful Savior—and what a wonderful salvation in Christ our Creator!

Don't delay. Please read and obey this verse of Scripture:

#set the
TONE

Jesus loves
you enough
to die on the
Cross for you.
Are you ready
to turn away
from sin and
live for Him?

"… If you confess with your mouth that Jesus is Lord and believe in your heart that God raised him from the dead, you will be saved" (Romans 10:9).

And when you have received this free gift of salvation, it is yours for eternity:

"I write these things to you who believe in the name of the Son of God, that you may know that you have eternal life" (1 John 5:13).

So, the next time you hear someone talking about human races, make sure to explain that there is only one human race—Adam's race. Tell them about the seven spiritual races, and do your best to help them understand how to make sure they're not a member of the "Lost Race."

We need to get out there and spread the wonderful news that God has told us the true history of the human race in His Word, the Bible. All humans are of one blood, one race. We all have the same problem—sin—and we all need same solution—to trust in the Lord Jesus Christ for salvation.

Related Scripture List:
Exodus 12:21-27
John 1:29
John 3:16
Romans 10:9
1 John 5:13
Revelation 21:1-4
Revelation 21:5-8
Revelation 21:22-27

CULTURE → A Call to Christ

Why does it matter what the real history of the world and people groups may be? It is important because it affects how we see our Creator and His plan for our life. It matters because it affects how we view ourselves, and more importantly, others.

At different points of history, there have been misguided and racist attempts to make some people groups more "civilized"—because people didn't see them as uniquely created and considered equal to themselves. Sadly, even some Christian leaders and missionaries in the past fell into this evolutionary, destructive thinking. Others considered it a "holy" mission to "civilize" indigenous peoples in areas colonized or ruled by so-called technologically and scientifically advanced nations.

This meant that many people groups were violently stripped of their native languages, social structure, family connections, ancestral lands—and forced to live a different life. Imagine how destructive it was for people to do this to others under the cruel impression this was needed and then try to share the gospel of Jesus Christ—who died to save people from all nations—with them. How different it is when those who are in missions reach out to indigenous people groups with respect and love as well as with the truth of Jesus Christ. Essentially, the missionary brings good news of salvation, so people are finally in a position to change any ungodly ways—cannibalism, child sacrifice—they may have had.

It's sad to see what damage and pain evolutionary thinking has caused throughout history and within the Church—and how it is so far away from what God made clear to us in His Word. We are all one race—one blood—all created in His image and loved by our Creator. We are all equal before God, all one family, all sinners in need of salvation.

Wow! The Bible tells us the history of people groups and how we are the descendants of Adam and Eve— so why is the question of "race" so complicated today?

The Bible makes it so simple: we are all one race—and all loved by God. People make it complicated with sin, and racism is simply a sin. When people see it for what it is, then we can really create change.

There are laws and educational programs to end racism—that is good—but that is not the real answer to eliminating it. Laws may change behaviors, education may change our thinking, but these don't solve where sin really lives—in our hearts.

Racism is hatred towards another person. People don't always show that or even say something that reveals the state of their heart. It can be invisible to the world, but not to God. He knows when we sin—and even if that sin is hidden in our heart, God still sees it.

Observational science helps us understand more about the world and ourselves, but it only shows what the Bible has said all along was true. So, if laws, education, and science aren't the answer, what is? Christ—He is the true answer for eliminating racism and division in our world today. In Him, we see the true equality that people are seeking. Knowing Christ and living by God's Word and how that applies to our everyday life is how we change the world. As you have learned about the real history of people, you learned about spiritual "races" too.

We see two spiritual races in the world today: those who believe in God's Word, accepting Christ as our Savior, and those who don't. Which one are you?

#set the
TONE

Observational science is where people study how things work through observing and measuring nature in the present.

The True Color of Christ

Jesus is often depicted as Caucasian, but He was most likely Middle Eastern in appearance.

When you think about Christ, how do you picture him? Most in their mind probably see Him as "Caucasian" in appearance because that is how He is often depicted. In reality, He probably looked more Middle Eastern in appearance. What is nice is that for most people they may never even wonder about what Christ looked like. They only see Him as our Savior, the Son of God, and our Redeemer. The color we associate most with Him is that of red—the color of His blood shed to save us from all our sins.

Blood is an interesting substance—there are four main types (A, B, AB, and O, and whether or not the protein called the Rh factor is present, our blood is either negative or positive). We inherit our blood type from the combination of genes from our parents. Some people groups may have slightly higher percentages of one type or another as well as some rare blood conditions. But our blood type isn't determined by "race."

During World War II in America, blood donations were segregated, which means separated, by the so-called "race" of the donor. The policy wasn't based on science, just the "racial" segregation practices in place at the time. An African American donor's blood could not be used for a 'Caucasian' of the same blood type. Thankfully, that wrong policy was soon ended.

Blood is important to us—both to our bodies and overall health. We cannot live without it. And we cannot live forever with God without accepting the blood of Christ as a sacrifice made for our sins. He suffered and died on the Cross, giving His own blood so that we would have the chance to have eternal life if we receive His powerful and loving gift. Remember, red is the only color that matters when you think of Christ. Have you received His gift of salvation? Would you like to?

Sin to Salvation

You now understand the true history of people and how this is revealed in the Bible. You know that all people are equal, racism is a sin, and anyone can commit this sin. You know that cultural differences are because of the Tower of Babel and family groups that left there to move throughout the world. Remember:

→ We are all uniquely and specially created by God.

→ We are all part of one race—the human race—and racism is a sin.

→ Jesus died on the Cross and became the Savior for each one of us.

If you haven't received the gift of salvation, and you no longer want to live without it, and you want to be part of the Lamb's Race, then I urge you to pray:

Jesus, please forgive me. I know You created me, and You died on the Cross for me and defeated death so I could live. I have sinned, I am a sinner, and I repent of my sins. I know You created me in Your image and love me as You sacrificed Your life for mine. I want to receive the gift of eternal life You offered me. Please live in my heart. I trust You and want You to be my Savior. In Your name, Amen.

Endnotes

1 "Adam + Eve = All Skin Tones?". 2016. Answers In Genesis. https://answersingenesis.org/racism/adam-eve-all-skin-tones/.

2 Purdom, Dr. Georgia. 2009. "The Amazing Regenerating Rib". Answers In Genesis. https://answersingenesis.org/human-body/the-amazing-regenerating-rib/.

3 Menton, Dr. David. 2010. "Melanin—Umbrellas Of Our Skin". Answers In Genesis. https://answersingenesis.org/human-body/melanin/.

4 Parker, Dr. Gary. 2016. "2.6 Variation, Yes; Evolution, No". Answers In Genesis. https://answersingenesis.org/creation-science/baraminology/variation-yes-evolution-no.

5 Ibid.

6 Pierce, Larry and Ken Ham. 2010. "Are There Gaps In The Genesis Genealogies?". Answers In Genesis. https://answersingenesis.org/bible-timeline/genealogy/gaps-in-the-genesis-genealogies/.

7 Purdom, Dr. Georgia and Dr. David Menton. 2010. "Did People Like Adam And Noah Really Live Over 900 Years?". Answers In Genesis. https://answersingenesis.org/bible-timeline/genealogy/did-adam-and-noah-really-live-over-900-years/.

8 "What Was The Pre-Flood Population Like?". 2016. Answers In Genesis. https://answersingenesis.org/noahs-ark/pre-flood-population/.

9 Hodge, Bodie. 2010. "Biblical Overview Of The Flood Timeline". Answers In Genesis. https://answersingenesis.org/bible-timeline/biblical-overview-of-the-flood-timeline/.

10 Ham, Ken. 2013. "Where Was The Garden Of Eden Located?". Answers In Genesis. https://answersingenesis.org/genesis/garden-of-eden/where-was-the-garden-of-eden-located/.

11 For more information: "Worldwide Flood, Worldwide Evidence". 2018. Answers In Genesis. https://answersingenesis.org/the-flood/global/worldwide-flood-evidence/; "The Flood And Fossils". 2016. Answers In Genesis. https://answersingenesis.org/kids/noahs-ark/flood-fossils/.

12 For more information, visit: Hodge, Bodie. 2007. "Why Don't We Find Human & Dinosaur Fossils Together?". Answers In Genesis. https://answersingenesis.org/dinosaurs/humans/why-dont-we-find-human-dinosaur-fossils-together/.

13 "Richard Loving". 2018. Biography. https://www.biography.com/people/richard-loving-110716.

14 Ham, Ken. 2008. "Interracial Marriage". Answers In Genesis. https://answersingenesis.org/family/marriage/interracial-marriage/

15 "Definition Of CULTURE". 2018. Merriam-Webster.com. https://www.merriam-webster.com/dictionary/culture.

16 For more information, visit: Foley, Avery. 2017. "Did Clothing Help Determine Our Shade Of Skin?". Answers In Genesis. https://answersingenesis.org/human-body/did-clothing-help-determine-our-shade-of-skin/.

17 "Definition Of RACE". 2018. Merriam-Webster.com. https://www.merriam-webster.com/dictionary/race.

18 "Ethnicity | Definition Of Ethnicity In US English By Oxford Dictionaries". 2018. Oxford Dictionaries | English. https://en.oxforddictionaries.com/definition/us/ethnicity.

19 Excerpted and adapted from: Hodge, Bodie, and Paul Taylor. 2015. "Doesn't The Bible Support Slavery?". Answers In Genesis. https://answersingenesis.org/bible-questions/doesnt-the-bible-support-slavery/.

20 Ibid.

21 Ibid.

22 Ibid.

23 Darwin, Charles. *The Descent of Man, and Selection in Relation to Sex.* New York: D. Appleton and Company, 1876, p. 156.

24 Mitchell, Dr. Tommy. 2009. "Darwin's Sacred Cause?". Answers In Genesis. https://answersingenesis.org/charles-darwin/racism/darwins-sacred-cause/.

25 "Johann Blumenbach And The Classification Of Human Races | Encyclopedia.com". 2001. Encyclopedia.com. https://www.encyclopedia.com/science/encyclopedias-almanacs-transcripts-and-maps/johann-blumenbach-and-classification-human-races. Accessed July 6, 2018.

26 Bhopal, Raj. "The Beautiful Skull and Blumenbach's Errors: The Birth of the Scientific Concept of Race." *British Medical Journal* 335.7633 (2007): 1308–1309. PMC. Web. 18 July 2018. https://www.ncbi.nlm.nih.gov/pmc/articles/PMC2151154/

27 For more information, visit: Hodge, Bodie. 2016. "The Results Of Evolution". Answers In Genesis. https://answersingenesis.org/sanctity-of-life/the-results-of-evolution/. Hall, Raymond. 2005. "Darwin's Impact—The Bloodstained Legacy Of Evolution". Answers In Genesis. https://answersingenesis.org/charles-darwin/racism/darwins-impact-the-bloodstained-legacy-of-evolution/. Mitchell, Dr. Elizabeth. 2012. "Human Evolution: Cause, Co-Conspirator, Or Cure For Racism?". Answers In Genesis. https://answersingenesis.org/charles-darwin/racism/belief-human-evolution-cause-conspirator-cure-racism/.

28 "Eugenics | Description, History, & Modern Eugenics". 2017. Encyclopedia Britannica. https://www.britannica.com/science/eugenics-genetics.

Photo and Illustration Credits:

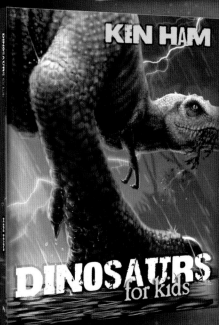

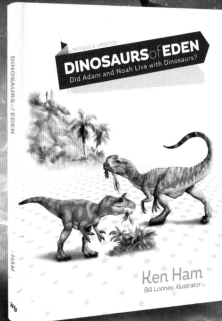

DINOSAURS FOR KIDS

Ken Ham

Within these pages kids will uncover the facts about dinosaur history from the creation to recent discoveries. Let Ken Ham take you on a journey through time to explore these awesome wonders of God's design.

978-0-89051-555-6 **$14.99** U.S.

DINOSAURS OF EDEN

Ken Ham

Fully revised and updated, this beloved classic will take you on a breathtaking trip across time to the biblical foundation of dinosaurs. This captivating adventure by Ken Ham explores the Garden of Eden, the exciting days of Noah's Flood, and the Tower of Babel. You'll learn the true history of the earth, and discover the very meaning and purpose of life!

978-0-89051-902-8 **$15.99** U.S.

WHAT REALLY HAPPENED TO THE DINOSAURS?

Ken Ham, John Morris

Travel side by side with Tracker John and his pet dinosaur DJ! Children will love the heartwarming story and fun-filled adventure. Adults will appreciate the scientific teaching of a biblical alternative.

978-0-89051-159-6 **$10.99** U.S.

Available where fine books are sold. MasterBooks.com

Master Books®
A Division of New Leaf Publishing Group
www.masterbooks.com